The IEA Health and Welfare Unit

Choice in Welfare No. 37

How to Pay for Health Care
Public and Private Alternatives

David Gladstone (editor)
Judith Allsop
Michael Goldsmith
David G. Green
Chris Ham

IEA Health and Welfare Unit
London

First published June 1997

The IEA Health and Welfare Unit
2 Lord North St
London SW1P 3LB

Learning from the Tigers: Stakeholder Health Care
© *The Lancet*, 1996

ISBN 0-255 36397-4
ISSN 1362-9565

Typeset by the IEA Health and Welfare Unit
in Bookman 10 point
Printed in Great Britain by
Hartington Fine Arts Ltd, Lancing, West Sussex

Contents

The Authors

David Gladstone is Director of Studies in Social Policy in the School for Policy Studies at the University of Bristol. He has recently edited *British Social Welfare: Past, Present and Future* and is also the editor of the Pioneers in Social Welfare series for Routledge and of the Introducing Social Policy series for the Open University Press.

Judith Allsop is Professor of Health Policy and Associate Director of the Social Sciences Research Centre at South Bank University. Her research interests are in lay views of health and illness; the regulation of professional work; complaining behaviour and dispute handling as well as health policy. Recent works include *Health Policy and the NHS: Towards 2000*, 1995 and *Regulating Medical Work: Formal and Informal Controls*, 1996, with L. Mulcahy.

Michael Goldsmith is Chief Executive of Sedgwick Noble Lowndes Health Consultancy. He is Chairman of the NHS Network, Vice Chairman of the Conservative Medical Society and an ex-NHS General Practitioner trainer. Dr Goldsmith has been a specialist policy adviser to successive Secretaries of State for Health and as such was intimately involved in the development of the 1990 NHS reforms. His most recent book is *Health to the People*, (with David Gladstone), 1996.

David Green is Director of the Health and Welfare Unit at the IEA. His books include *Working-Class Patients and the Medical Establishment*, 1985; *The New Right*, 1987; *Reinventing Civil Society*, 1993; and *Community Without Politics*, 1996.

Chris Ham is Director of the Health Services Management Centre at the University of Birmingham. He works with Health Authorities and NHS Trusts on the implementation of the NHS reforms, and his research interests include priority setting in health services and health care reform in the international context. His books include *Health Check*, 1990; *Health Policy in Britain*, 1992 third edition; and *Management and Competition in the NHS*, 1997.

iv

Editor's Introduction

Health Care Funding:
Some History and Issues

David Gladstone

IT WAS just over fifty years ago—in November 1946—that the Bill creating the National Health Service received the Royal Assent; although the service itself did not come into operation until the Appointed Day, 5 July 1948. With its promise of health care free to the user at the point of demand, the NHS soon acquired strong popular support. It was seen as the 'jewel in the crown' of the social legislation of the 1940s, the centre-piece of Britain's welfare state. Rudolf Klein neatly captures its distinctive significance:

> It was the first health system in any Western society to offer free medical care to the entire population. At the time of its creation it was a unique example of the collectivist provision of health care in a market society.[1]

One of the assumptions on which the NHS was based was that once the backlog of ill health had been treated, demand would reduce and the service would settle into a steady state. That proved a chimera; and one of the recurrent issues for the NHS has been to equate supply and demand in the absence of price. The problems began early in its history. Demand outstripped available resources. Bevan, the Minister of Health, spoke to the Parliamentary Labour Party of 'cascades of medicine pouring down British throats—and they're not even bringing the bottles back'.[2] Meanwhile, supplementary estimates for the NHS threatened the post-devaluation economy drive, and authority to introduce prescription charges was announced in October 1949 (thought they were not introduced until 1952). The imposition of a ceiling on health service spending, however, together with the introduction of dental charges and charges for spectacles in

1

1951, finally precipitated Aneurin Bevan's resignation as Minister of Health. Despite these attempts to contain cost and increase revenue, the political concern with the financing of the NHS did not go away. In 1953 a Committee of Inquiry was appointed chaired by the Cambridge economist Claude Guillebaud. Its Report, published in 1956, suggested that much of the alarm about the extravagance of the NHS had been misplaced.[3] Much of the apparent increase in spending was due, the Report suggested, to general price inflation, while earlier spending crises were now effectively under control.

What the Guillebaud Committee failed to address, however, were the long term problems of an ageing population and rising expectations. Together with vast improvements in medical research and health technology they have been inter-related strands in an on-going political concern with potentially limitless demand on the one hand and finite resources on the other.

The demand-side factors are, of course, by no means peculiar or unique to Britain. They are common features facing health care systems world-wide, as successive international reports have demonstrated.[4] In a publicly funded health care system, however, they inevitably bring into play wider economic consider-ations: about the scale of funding regarded as appropriate, the share of public expenditure allocated and the tax burden that is necessary. In a National Health Service these are inescapably political decisions. But in any matter to do with health they shade into moral choice: about the worth of individuals, access to resources and the efficacy or outcome of particular treatment regimes.

What governments can do in relation to demand factors is limited; but there is greater room for manoeuvre on supply-side issues. Successive governments have initiated measures involv-ing one or more of the following strategies. First, they may attempt to increase revenue. Prescription charges, charges for particular aspects of health care such as dental and ophthalmic services or for specific elements of service such as charges for amenity beds or 'private' rooms are all revenue-raising methods. So too is the sale of 'surplus' NHS landholdings and Nurses Homes as well as the franchising of shops in NHS hospital premises.

Secondly, governments may attempt to cut costs. Waiting lists for treatment constituted an important indicative method of rationing resources by reducing demand. As such, they may serve to cut costs in the short-term—if not the long-term. With the introduction of new service standards in the Patient's Charter and the reduction of waiting lists that has been created, there is currently a heightening of tension between what is expected and what can be delivered.

Thirdly, governments may attempt to maximise efficiency in the use of resources. This has been the objective of the various administrative reorganisations to which the NHS has been subjected, and it also lay behind the introduction of a general management system into the NHS in 1983. At that time one critic lamented that management arrangements in the NHS were so complex that if Florence Nightingale were to return to a late twentieth century hospital she would be searching in vain for the person in charge.[5] The introduction of the internal (or quasi) market in the NHS reforms of 1990 split the functions of providing services from those of purchasing.[6] The so-called purchaser/provider split was itself part of an attempt to create a more efficiently competitive service. One consequence of that innovation has been an increase in the number of bureaucrats and managers, an issue of which much has been made by the critics of the reforms. That, however, should not distract attention from the need for good management within the NHS. Management—both of human and financial resources—is central to the delivery of high quality patient care and essential in an organisation which currently spends approximately £40 billion of taxation revenue and which remains the largest employer in Western Europe.

Each of the contributors to this collection was asked to address the issue of health service finance in the light of the trends which have just been outlined, and to reflect on alternative scenarios for the future.

For Allsop, speculation about future patterns of morbidity and new treatments and therapies leads her to conclude (p. 14) that 'the case for moving away from a centrally planned, free at the point of service, NHS has little to offer'. But her defence of the basic principles of the traditional or classic NHS is also grounded on three arguments: moral, economic and social. Morally she argues (p. 11) that 'the justification for public spending on maintaining and promoting good health and supplying medical services for both care and cure can be justified in terms of social justice and equality both of opportunity and outcome'. Economically the case for a 'free' service rests both on positive and negative factors. The positive factors include the collective as well as individual benefits that health programmes produce, the contribution which they make to a healthy and productive workforce and the lower administrative and management costs compared to those in more competitive insurance-based schemes. The experience of higher administrative costs that occur when insurers compete for business is one of the factors Ham refers to in discussing the negative factors of the health care markets (p. 24). Others he mentions are 'the risk that insurers will engage in adverse selections, and the disincentive that applies for individuals to stay healthy or keep their use of health services to minimum if they are fully insured against the cost of treatment'. Allsop's third argument in favour of maintaining a NHS free to the user is based on social solidarity. 'The common experience of contributing to, and using, a service which is open to everyone', she contends, 'adds to the sense of community'. The role of the NHS in creating and reinforcing social cohesion is one of David Green's starting points. But whereas that defence leads Allsop to favour a centrally planned service, Green sees a more limited role for governance. There can be solidarity, he argues, without public-sector monopoly (p. 30). His view is that there is no need for government to be responsible for both funding and provision. Instead the role of government action should be confined to ensuring that everyone has access to an agreed level and standard of care. Green has previously been an advocate of private insurance alternatives to a state-funded NHS. In this essay, however, he admits some of the criticisms that have been made of that position and opts instead for a modified version of Enthoven's scheme of managed competition. With the purchaser/provider split, Enthoven's ideas played a significant role in the development of the quasi-market arrangements introduced into the NHS in April 1991. His latest ideas emphasise the role of agencies managing consumer choice 'by offering competitive information about quality and price and by filtering out unsatisfactory insurers who try to compete by selecting good risks rather than encouraging cost-effective care' (p. 51). How such a scheme would become operational in Britain is the theme of the final section of Green's paper. In a nutshell it would require a transformation in the role of health authorities and hospitals, changes in the activities of private insurers and a more formal process of consumer choice.

Michael Goldsmith examines the case for charges in the NHS, in addition to those which already exist. He indicates what he considers the 'three most obvious areas' (p. 19) where such charges a might be introduced. These are for visits to the GP, for outpatient services and hotel charges for in-patients. Their potential, he believes, is limited. Goldsmith's own figures suggest that if each of them was to be introduced, together they would produce below £2 billion per year which, as he pointed out, is only equal to what the NHS has to grow by on an annual basis to keep pace with fiscal and medical inflation. His conclusion, therefore, is that although new charges may appear superficially attractive, they offer little new potential. Because of that, 'other methods of health financing will need to be introduced if the government is to sustain the NHS in its present form without resorting to considerable increases in taxation' (p. 22).

These three papers all draw comparisons between the British experience and the health care and financial arrangements of other countries. But such comparisons are central to Chris Ham's contribution which is a reprint of an article originally published in *The Lancet* in April 1996. His focus is on Singapore which, as he sees it, represents 'a middle way between a *laissez-faire* system and a government-regulated national health service' (p. 23). There are considerable similarities between Green's ideas and Ham's discussion of the Singapore model. Both, for example, envisage primarily a regulatory role for government. In Singapore that extends to health service delivery as well as to finance. But where Singapore's medisave is a savings—rather than an insurance—scheme, Green envisages in his model a continuing—though changed—role for the private insurance sector. As Ham indicates, current British interests in the Singaporean model goes beyond its specific framework for heath care. That is only one part of a new and more comprehensive set of arrangements in economic relations and welfare services that is encapsulated in the term 'stakeholder'.

The use of that term in the essays by Allsop, Green and Ham suggest its contemporary significance in discussions of health policy, though it is appropriate to remember that the specific meanings attached to it may vary. It does, however, serve to highlight two sets of relationships which are integral to the

essays in this collection. First of these is the changing relationship of medical professionals, managers and users in the modern
health care system. The second is the relationship between
health funding and the broader politico-economic context within
which such decisions are taken. Part of Allsop's future scenario
is a recognition of the inter-relationship between health and
other aspects of welfare policy. This entails not only health care
target-setting but the pursuit of other policy objectives: 'for
employment, for training, for income-maintenance, particularly
for families with children, and an incomes policy which aims to
reduce income differentials' (p. 14). Meanwhile Ham highlights
the economic factors that have produced Singapore's distinctive
model:

> An economy which has grown by around 8.5 per cent a year since
> gaining independence and which provides full employment has
> enabled the government to require individuals to save to meet the
> costs of medical care, pensions and other needs. An economy with
> lower levels of employment would have had to rely much more on
> government funding, if only to provide a safety net for the poor. The
> most important lesson is that a stakeholder welfare system must grow
> out of a stakeholder economy rather than vice versa. (p. 29)

The essays in this collection suggest lessons from the past and
lessons from elsewhere, a willingness to analyse and evaluate, to
defend and propose. They offer a number of alternative routes
that lead beyond the present system into a more user-responsive
and financially responsible health care system.

Why Health Care Should Be Provided Free at the Point of Service

Judith Allsop

Introduction

THIS PAPER argues that health services should be provided free at the point of use within the framework of a centrally planned service. It begins by outlining the changing social context within which the NHS operates and the recent changes in its structure. It then reviews the moral, economic and social arguments and concludes with an assessment of the main challenges facing policy makers and providers for which market forces offer no solutions.

The Changing Context of the NHS

The NHS as it was set up in 1948 aimed to exclude market forces from the provision of health and medical care. The purpose of the service was to provide care free at the point of use when it was needed, for rich and poor alike. The service was funded from general taxation, centrally organised with provision at the local level determined by boards with appointed members who represented the professionals working in the service and the local community. Policies and priorities were determined nationally and implemented locally to meet local needs.

From the 1970s, the NHS came under increasing criticism. Both primary care and the preventive services had suffered from policy neglect while policy for the caring services had been riddled with perverse incentives and implementation problems. Both the political right and left have criticised NHS under-funding, the shortfalls in service due to rising demand, the insensitivity to patient needs and the influence exercised by the bureaucratic and professional hospital-based élites within the NHS. In the wake of the financial crises of the late 1970s, Conservative governments were determined to reduce public spending and introduce more business-like practices in the public sector. In the NHS, levels of growth slowed and failed to keep pace with demand. The rising numbers of elderly people whose need for medical care is high, new technologies and the need for renewal have created a constant pressure on the health budget. As a consequence, the mid-1980s saw crisis management; growing waiting lists and public dissatisfaction. Deregulation and privatisation were used to introduce private sector principles into the service. The optical services were largely excluded from the NHS, and many dentists have moved into private practice. Support services in the hospital sector were subject to tender and there was a rapid growth in private care for people with disabilities, the elderly and frail.

In 1990 the NHS reforms were introduced to produce a more cost effective NHS while retaining the principle of a tax-funded service free at the point of use. The split between local purchasers—health authorities and GPs—who have cash-limited budgets and the trusts, who must win contracts to provide services, brought market forces into the supply of NHS services. Items of service must be costed and priced by trusts who must win contracts from purchasers to remain financially viable. Purchasers may seek tenders from the private sector. Private sector finance may be sought to provide capital for NHS building, and facilities may also be under private sector management. Although research on the new NHS has been limited, these supply-side changes have led to increased diversity and variability of provision and greater uncertainty and inequity for patients.[1] The planning function has been weakened and, inevitably, there are costs associated with contracting so that management now takes a higher proportion of the NHS budget.

Those on the right have argued that more fundamental changes are necessary. They have focussed on the lack of choice for health care users. Access can be barred by professionals who determine entry to the health system. They have also argued that the level of expenditure on private health care is low in the UK. And the standard of care, particularly in the chronic illness services, is well below that in the US and other EU countries. People may be inhibited in decisions about how much to spend on their own health care because the NHS is so dominant. Some critics argued that the availability of free health services actually encourages unhealthy lifestyles as there are no costs associated with ill health. It has also been argued that the marketisation of supply, the encouragement of private insurance and user charges would both raise revenue and increase freedom of choice. While these criticisms may have some foundation, do they lead to the conclusion that further marketisation would address the problems?

The next stage of NHS development is uncertain. On the one hand, the supply of health services could be privatised further with hospitals and GP practices owned by companies and managed to provide a profit in the style of health maintenance organisations (HMOs) in the US. This would restrict what was available to patients on the basis of the terms of their particular HMO. It would increase diversity further, bring a patch-work quilt of provision and do nothing to improve services in poorer areas. National insurance, private insurance or a mixed system are alternatives to tax-based funding. However, in these systems, administrative costs rise and there is a loss of equity. In the light of a possible policy shift in this direction, the moral, economic and social arguments for a health service free at the point of use are reviewed.

Health and Health Care Needs: the Moral Case

Health is a basic human need, perhaps the most basic, as poor health can deprive the individual of any capacity for agency through early death, or limit it as a consequence of chronic sickness or disability. On the other hand, good health, as we know from a number of studies, is seen by people to bring a sense of balance, of equilibrium and of wellbeing.[2] Such a sense of wellbeing can be taken as an end in itself as well as enhancing an individual's ability to adapt and change to meet new challenges. For this reason, the provision of health services without direct charge has been seen as a moral imperative. If human beings are seen as having equal rights to the exercise of agency, then, in a social democracy, it is incumbent on the state to use collective resources to ensure that good health is maintained; that there is easy access to medical services when people are ill; and that those who are in need of care because they are frail or disabled receive help and support. If the claims to social justice are to be met, then universal access and a concern for equality of outcome follow.

A further moral argument is that illness or disability can strike at any time and incur high costs for the individual. They can bring pain and suffering and a loss in the capacity to earn which affects the person concerned, their close family, dependents and friends. Moreover, if medical care must be paid for, the costs may exceed an individual's capacity to pay. For this reason, most relatively wealthy societies have some mechanism to pool the risks of individual illness. A tax-based system which provides open access to health care at the point of need has the greatest capacity to ensure that appropriate care is received. It can reduce anxiety for the individual and an equitable distribution of good quality services can be achieved through central planning.

There is ample evidence that ill health is socially patterned and not necessarily the consequence of an individual's actions. Ill health is generally due to a variety of factors such as genetic endowment, material and environmental conditions as well as individual behaviour. The precise relationship between these factors in the case of particular individuals is difficult to unravel as they may have a complex interactional effect over a lifetime. On the basis of data available, it is rarely possible to attribute causal factors in illness and early death unequivocally. However, research reports from the nineteenth century Blue Books, which studied the effects of industrial processes on health, to contemporary analyses of social class and ill health have shown consistently that those who live and work in poorer material circumstances have worse health.[3] Moreover, there is a social class gradient with a difference by a factor of three in health care outcomes between the highest and lowest social groups using a number of measures. Even where poverty is not an issue, longitudinal studies of different grades of British civil servant demonstrated a gradient in terms of mortality rates from the lowest group of clerical grades, who had the worst mortality rates, to the highest grades, who had the best.[4] It is not known with certainty why these differences occur but it could be that the lack of autonomy and the under-use of people's capacities could themselves increase susceptibility to illness.

Some have argued that ill health may be a consequence of individual choice. However, while those who smoke, abuse alcohol or drugs or fail to follow other basic principles of healthy living contribute to their own ill health, it can rarely be attributed solely to individual actions. Behaviours are often related to other material factors which affect the ability to exercise agency and are adopted to cope with stress and uncertainty, rather than the other way round. There is evidence to support a cycle of ill health. Poverty due to ill health can affect children and their capacity for growth and development. There is strong evidence that poor material circumstances and poor nurturing can increase susceptibility to illness and disease in later life.

In sum, an appropriate moral stance would be that healthy environments and access to medical care should be provided by the social group so that the costs which follow from ill health do not lie where they fall. Those who are less materially well off will be doubly disadvantaged if they also have to pay for their care. Conversely, those who enjoy good health are in a strong position to obtain other material advantages, particularly within capitalist societies. Therefore, the justification for public spending on maintaining and promoting good health and supplying medical services for both cure and care can be justified in terms of social justice and equality of both opportunity and outcome.

The Economic Case

There are also a number of economic arguments for services without direct payment. There are benefits to the collectivity as a whole from promoting good health and controlling diseases which are referred to by economists as externalities. Public health measures such as vaccination and immunisation programmes can bring collective benefits through group immunity to diseases such as smallpox, cholera, german measles, whooping cough, polio and so on. Policies to prevent the spread of HIV/AIDS and efforts to prevent a resurgence of TB, salmonella and the like, can be justified in terms of both individual and collective benefit. To charge for such services would bring disbenefits and waste human resources.

Moreover societies, particularly capitalist ones, require a productive workforce. In a well known example from the past, it was the poor health of the Boer War recruits which led to proposals for free school meals and medical services in the early part of the twentieth century. Although general health status is now better, high rates of sick-leave from work can still impair the efficiency of public services and cut the profit margins of private sector business. In an era of rapid technological change, the capacity to adapt is crucial. Poor health among employees can lead to apathy and disinterest as well as absence from work.

Good health may even be a factor in international competitiveness. To take an example from the present day, it has been pointed out that Japan moved very rapidly from low levels of economic development and limited life expectancy to the longest life expectancy in the world and very high levels of economic growth.[5] Wilkinson points to the relative income equality in Japan compared to the UK.[6] Indeed, as income differentials in the UK have widened, so have differentials in morbidity and mortality. While it is difficult to disentangle cause and effect, it is clear that good health and longevity, adequate material conditions and economic growth tend to go together.

The benefits of a centrally planned and tax-funded system of health care where facilities are owned by the state can also be argued on the basis of value for money. The administrative and management costs in the NHS, even after the 1990 health reforms, remain low compared to insurance-based systems. Moreover, such a system can be geared to setting policies and priorities for health care spending within a global budget which represents what the country can afford.

Compared to collective ownership, in a market system of health care, private capital inevitably seeks profit. Private suppliers are likely to avoid high cost, specialist care where there is low demand but where there is a high research and development cost. Neither can the private sector be expected to be committed to ensuring national coverage or equity in access and outcome. On the demand side, user charges deter people seeking medical attention, even if there is clinical need. Private insurance, in the economist's term, 'cream skims'. It selects the best risks—that is, the healthiest—and often limits cover to exclude high cost care. Under such a system inequities in the distribution of health care and the differences in health care outcomes would be likely to increase. Moreover, market forces tend to operate to fulfill short-term individual wants rather than long-term investment in the collective interest. It is possible that the demand for medical services would increase at the expense of the less dramatic primary and preventive care sectors.

The Social Solidarity Argument

A further instrumental reason for universality of provision of health and medical services without charge was put forward by Titmuss and remains central to Fabian socialism.[7] Titmuss suggested that the common experience of contributing to, and using, a service which is open to everyone adds to the sense of community. It can prevent alienation and integrate minority groups and regional cultures into broader societal norms and values. The pooling of risks can encourage altruism, strengthen social relationships and bring a sense of belonging to a welfare society. Indeed this approach has led neo-Marxists to argue that the decommodification of state services bolsters and renews capitalism as there are functional benefits in terms of reproduction and legitimation.[8] Certainly, the NHS has been a popular public service commanding widespread support.

The social solidarity argument has another aspect. Health systems rely on expert labour. While expert groups are organised into professional associations with codes of ethics which put a concern for the service-recipients' interests to the fore, the profit motive creates incentives for personal gain. It has been a mark of the NHS that, on the whole, professionals have been motivated by a concern for the best interests of the patient, and have determined priorities on the basis of the greatest need within the resources available.

Health Needs in the Twenty-first Century

In the twenty-first century, there is no reason to suppose that the pattern of illness will change markedly. Particularly if smoking remains a common practice, heart disease and the cancers will lead to deaths before their time. Accidents will continue to take their toll and chronic illness, mental illness and disability will create major demands for care. At least for the next decade, the numbers of elderly people will continue to rise.

On the supply side, there is no reason to think that new therapies will not continue to develop. Some innovations, particularly in drug therapies and less invasive surgery, may lead to cheaper care. New information technologies have increased the capacity of managers to compare the performance of hospitals, units and doctors and to tackle some of the variations in performance and practice. Databases provide the technology to assess the results of clinical trials in medical centres across the globe and it is becoming easier to identify treatments which are cost-effective. Managers in trusts and purchasers in health authorities have been urged to use such findings to assess which services to purchase for their local population.

In the context of these changes and in the light of the moral, economic and social arguments cited above, the case for moving away from a centrally-planned, free-at-the-point-of-service, NHS has little to offer. Of necessity, governments must take a lead in promoting health through public policy. This requires not only setting targets for reducing the incidence of particular diseases but also pursuing a range of welfare goals through policies for employment, for training, for income-maintenance, particularly for families with children, and an incomes policy which aims to reduce income differentials. Only governments have the powers required to control health hazards and promote healthy lifestyles through giving a steer to public policy. Experience in North America suggests that local alliances are necessary. These imply shared aims and a degree of social solidarity. Canada in partic- ular has developed a policy framework and a variety of participative structures for health promotion and the care of the chronically ill. Norway's policy of subsidy to healthy foods and high taxation on unhealthy ones provides a way of promoting health indirectly through public action rather than trying to change individual behaviour.[9]

Policies for good primary care, free at the point of service, are also essential to ensure intervention at the earliest stage and to ensure that knowledge and information about self-care are readily available. Because, in the first instance, people take the decision themselves to seek medical help, a trusting and co- operative relationship between people and their primary-care practitioners is important. Even in countries where GNP per head is low, effective primary care, free of charge, is seen as a priority.[10] It is cost-effective as it provides a filter to more expensive high-cost treatment. The challenge lies in developing structures for service delivery by a range of professionals in a way which involves local communities, rather than in imposing charges which may limit access. GP practices require good management and this can achieve the organisation of patient demand without the necessity for user charges.

In relation to the hospital services, the purchaser/provider split has the advantage of a separation of roles between managers in trusts and purchasers in health authorities and GP practices. The first can concentrate on providing cost-effective services while the latter can assess population needs. The health reforms have made choices more transparent through the costing and pricing of services. However, there is no intrinsic reason why contracting should not take place within a collaborative framework. Further marketisation of the NHS will not provide solutions to the main problems, which are the following:

- How to determine local needs and services
- How to incorporate budget-holding GPs into health authority purchasing, thereby combining the knowledge which GPs have of their patients with the requirements of the local population in general
- How to involve local populations in determining health care needs without ignoring minority groups
- How to maintain highly specialist centres of excellence where costs are high and demand is on a national, rather than a local basis

It is beyond the scope of this short paper to find answers to these problems. In a centrally planned, tax-based, free-at-the-point-of-service system, the onus lies on the various stakeholders to find creative solutions for promoting and maintaining health, as well as curing and caring for the sick. The moral and economic arguments for doing so and the advantages in terms of social cohesion remain as strong at the end of the twentieth century as they were for the social reformers at its beginning.

Co-payment: A Vehicle for NHS Funding Enhancement?

Michael Goldsmith

IN BRITAIN since 1948 the National Health Service has been funded on the basis that care is largely free at the point of service. The intention of the Beveridge report of 1942, which preceded the NHS Act of 1946, was that all health care would be provided free of charge by the state. The Act succeeded in bringing this about for the first time in British history. However, this idyll did not last long and fear of unbridled expense caused the Labour government under Attlee to legislate for the introduction of prescription charges in 1949. It had been thought amongst others by Aneurin Bevan, the then Minister of Health, that the increase in health status brought about by a largely free health service would be paid for and balanced out by the reduction in costs to the state of 'curing' existing diseases. This was already shown to be fallacious by the time that the introduction of dental and prescription charges led to huge conflicts within the Labour Party. Hugh Gaitskell, the then Chancellor of the Exchequer, wanted a lid on fiscal policy and health service spending. This led to violent disagreements within the Cabinet and the resignation of Aneurin Bevan, on a point of principle. Two others left the Cabinet at the same time: Harold Wilson, a future Labour Prime Minister, and John Freeman.

Although the electorate has periodically moaned about the inexorable rise of prescription charges, the fact remains that the elderly, the very young and the chronic sick are vulnerable groups who are exempt from these charges. Traditionally there have been groups of chronic diseases like diabetes, thyroid disease and various forms of colitis for which regular medications are required and for which exemption from charges is given. Children are exempt until their eighteenth birthday and all pensioners are similarly exempt. Given that the remainder of adults on regular medications can take out a 'season ticket' which caps their annual prescription spend, the actual burden on working adults at £5.65 per item is not onerous. There has been a general acceptance of NHS charges as an additional source of NHS finance and, currently, approximately three per cent of the annual NHS budget is provided by prescription charges.

The problem with increasing these charges above the existing levels is that the major burden falls upon that proportion of the working population who are chronically ill or poor. This produces inequalities and limits the range and scope of the population who are actually paying. In theory it also may discourage patients from seeking treatment because of the potential financial burden. However, conversely, it has been shown that increasing the prescription charge encourages more of the population to buy medication privately for rates cheaper than the NHS charge. This reduces the overall national prescribing bill.

Other examples of patient charges which are currently in use include dental fees which have increased five-fold between 1980 and 1991. The onset of realistic dental charges has reduced NHS dental demand by making the costs of NHS dentistry more like that of the private sector and encouraging the take-up of private dental insurance. Many employers are now offering either company-paid dental insurance benefits or a voluntary scheme sponsored by the company. Other employers are providing an in-house dental service at the workplace by employing a dentist privately.

It is my view that the dental model of patient charging is not appropriate for the medical model because dental health is generally more static and less prone to sudden disabling and expensive illness. Some sets of charges have actually been damaging both to the government's reputation and probably to the patients' health. In particular this is true of the abolition of free eye-tests by the Thatcher government in 1989. Recent research has shown that rates of untreated glaucoma may actually have risen because of the disincentive to preventative eye care caused by the charges.[1]

Charges In Other Countries

So what do other countries do in relation to charges for state-provided health care? In New Zealand recent health reforms, not dissimilar to those in the UK, have also produced some form of rationing. New Zealand has chosen to reduce the range of services available in order to ensure as wide a degree of coverage in the population as possible.

Medical, pharmaceutical and hospital benefits are directed to three income levels—Groups 1, 2 + 3. People in Groups 1 + 2 get free hospital and GP care. However, Group 3 patients face a $16 charge for children and $31 for adults. The first five outpatient visits for a family also have to be paid for by the family. There is a prescription charge of $5 per item for people in Groups 1 + 2 and also for adults and children who are 'heavy users' of health care. People in Group 3 pay up to $15 per item for adults and $10 per item for children. Certain medicines are also subject to an additional manufacturers' premium charge to the patient. Doctors and chemists have a list of these items.

In Germany, those with salary levels over about £35,000 are required to take out private insurance instead of using the Krankenkasse system of free health care, financed by employers' and employees' contributions. The Krankenkasse is literally an illness bank and is a type of insurance where employees and employers pay contributions into an insurer linked to that particular industry (e.g. car workers, farm workers, etc.). The Krankenkasse then pays out to doctors and hospitals according to a nationally agreed formulary and protocol of charges and procedures and treatments. Fees are negotiated by the medical profession every two or three years with government approval and price-fixing. Here too there is some co-payment for subscription charges. Under the 1989 Health Reform Act, the German government introduced a system of reference prices which has meant that, although manufacturers of medicines are still free to set their own prices, if these exceed the reference prices set down by the government, the patient has to pay the difference. This 'encourages' patients to select cheaper generic products so as to try to avoid co-payment.

In France, only 30 per cent of chronic diseases are treated for free. A fee of about 35FF per day is levied for hospital treatment, although the poor and indigent are exempt. 'Life-saving' drugs are free but a contribution is levied for 'comfort' medicines. Patients have to pay the GP or dentist for services and then obtain an 80 per cent re-imbursement from the state health insurance office. Most major companies in France subscribe to group medical insurance plans for employees and their families. 80 per cent of individuals in France have some form of medical insurance cover. These private plans are usually intended to cover the top-up moderateur, i.e. the sum of the medical treatment not reimbursed by the state.

New Types of Charges

So what other types of charge or co-payment might be considered in a review of income generation for the NHS? The three most obvious areas concern charges for visits to the GP, charges for outpatient services and hotel charges for inpatients.

GP visit charges

Some people argue that small charges for going to see a GP are not only revenue generating but also beneficial. They may actually reduce the number of repetitive or frivolous consultations whilst making patients 'value' the consultation more. For some time, GPs who practise privately have stated anecdotally that payment for a consultation enhances the 'value' of the consultation for the patient because he is handing over hard-earned money for it and at the same time the GP is under a professional contract to give value for money.

Conversely, many GPs argue that payment for consultations would be risky because it might put off patients from seeking help because of financial constraints and thus endanger early presentation of serious conditions. In other words a patient might delay seeking advice for a non-specific condition (eg a lump) and the condition thus be worsened and make subsequent treatment more expensive for the NHS.

Outpatient service charges

Similar arguments can be made for and against charges made for attending hospital outpatients. The argument that patients may not attend because of cost are less strong, however, because they will have been already referred by their GP and they know that their GP will be aware if they fail to attend. It can also be said that unnecessary repeat referrals would be kept to a minimum. The costs of collection of such charges would, however, be high unless the system mitigated for cash levies on arrival at either the GP surgery or outpatient clinic. The precedent of patients regularly paying such charges at their NHS dentist already exists.

Hotel charges

One of the most contentious ideas for NHS co-payment is that of charging for hotel services in hospitals. Clearly this is a highly emotive and politically sensitive area. One can envisage headlines such as: 'Government impose charges on the sick and dying' or 'Government to punish the sick'.

However, the fact remains that patients who are admitted to hospital from their own homes are then receiving free board and lodging which they would have had to pay for at home. Unfortunately the political sensitivity and the combination of the costs of collection and the fact that hospital stays are getting shorter make this a weak sources of income.

What Income Might These Charges Bring In?

Some examples of the amounts of revenue that these ideas might raise are given below:

1 *GP charges*

At £5 per visit, with an average of four visits per year per patient, charges for visiting the GP would raise approximately £1 billion (the same as prescription charges presently).

2 *Prescription charges*

Extending charges to higher income households (by cancelling exemptions) would raise £350 million per year.

3 *Outpatient charges*

Charging £10 per outpatient visit for the 15 million consultations which take place annually would produce £150 million per year.

4 *Hotel charges*

A £10 charge per day could raise approximately £200 million. This would increase to £500 million if a £10 per day-case were levied.

Even if all these ideas were developed into a co-payment health policy by the government, the total revenue, at most, would be about £2 billion. This is just over five per cent of the total NHS expenditure for 1996/7 of £38 billion and equal only to about what the NHS has to grow by on an *annual* basis to keep pace with fiscal and medical inflation. Most governments would believe that a five per cent contribution would not be sufficient to weather the political storm which would probably surround the development of such a policy.

Conclusion

Introducing new co-payments or increasing charges which already exist are a superficially attractive proposition. I have shown that an overall increase in revenue of about five per cent of the total NHS budget might be achieved by introducing a range of charges surrounding all aspects of NHS care. Not withstanding the attraction of introducing new money from the people to a service which is quintessentially always demanding more cash, the political risks to any party of such a policy are manifest.

The NHS has always been something of a sacred cow in Britain. It has been seen as essentially a free service by the people and has always been available largely free at the point of delivery without the requirement of an ability to pay. Prescription, dental and ophthalmic charges have appeared to the public to be a minor nuisance and the protection of the very young, the elderly and the unwaged has meant that only those who 'can afford it' have had to pay anything towards health care.

Furthermore the public always view the NHS as being paid for through their National Insurance contributions and there is a natural aversion to 'paying twice'. Many a GP has groaned inwardly when a patient complains about service quoting the well worn epithet 'I pay my stamp'. The fact is that the NHS is financed mainly through direct taxation and not through the National Insurance contributions which do not even finance Social Security let alone Health.

The popular perception about the public financing of the NHS makes it really difficult for any government to introduce new charges. On top of this the sociological and medical arguments already rehearsed above mean that most doctors would fight against charges because of the chances of altering the balance of need versus provision. If patients felt they could save money by not using the service the charges would become a voluntary health tax and might well affect public health outcomes. Indeed in other countries, and in private health insurance, co-payments are used for reducing health demands as well as increasing contribution from the public.

The principles of equality, access and the perception of the people about their National Health Service need to be analysed in relation to co-payment. The NHS is a fantastically popular institution and engenders an almost nationalistic fervour amongst British politicians. There has been an understanding between the government and the people since 1948 that access to health care would be on an equal basis regardless of colour, creed, or ability to pay. The increased imposition therefore of co-payment starts to eat into the 'regardless of ability to pay' elements of the unwritten NHS charter. Most sociologists would agree that the need to pay money directly for health care on a fee-for-service basis obviously hits the poor more than the wealthy and also, for the first time since 1948, forces the people to make financial choices on spending on health care which previously had all been made for them. Whilst I am not unhappy about the latter, I am uncomfortable about the former.

In conclusion, therefore, I do not favour the introduction of any new NHS charges at this time. The imposition of any new charges would convey the wrong message from the government and would give the impression that the NHS was lurching away from its founding tenets that health care be delivered free at the point of service regardless of the means of the individual. Other methods of health financing will need to be introduced if the government is to sustain the NHS in its present form without resorting to considerable increases in taxation.

Learning from the Tigers: Stakeholder Health Care

Chris Ham

IMAGINE A country which provides health care for only three per cent of its gross domestic product. Imagine a country which achieves population health outcomes as good as those of the OECD countries. Imagine a country where a partnership between government and its citizens ensures access to basic medical care for all. This country is not a figment of a deranged health policy analyst's imagination. It is real and it is called Singapore.

Known more for the success of its economy than its health service, Singapore is attracting increasing interest among health policy makers on both sides of the Atlantic. The reason is simple. Singapore's system of compulsory medical savings accounts and government subsidies appears to offer a remarkably effective way of financing health care. At a time when other options for reform have either failed or are running out of steam, the experience of Singapore repays study as an alternative way of financing and delivering health care.

Put simply, Singapore has chosen a middle way between a *laissez-faire* system and a government-regulated national health service. A free market in health care has been rejected because of the well known sources of market failure in health care. These include the risk that insurers will engage in adverse selection, the disincentive for individuals to stay healthy or minimise their use of health services if they are fully insured against the cost of

We are very grateful to the Editor for permission to reprint this article which was first published in *The Lancet*, 6 April 1996, Vol. 347, No. 9006, pp. 951-53.

treatment, and the high administrative costs that arise when insurers compete for business.

Recognition of these problems has led the Singaporean government to intervene to regulate the provision of facilities, medical manpower and the flow of funds. As far as financing is concerned, citizens are required to save a proportion of their income each month, with the money being put into a medical savings account known as Medisave. Currently this involves payments of around three per cent of income for those aged under 35 increasing to four per cent for people over 45 years of age. The contribution of workers is matched by employers.

Contributions are tax exempt and they accumulate over a lifetime. The resulting savings are drawn on to pay for the costs of medical care and to build up reserves for use in old age when people stop work. Money set aside in Medisave accounts earns interest and contributions continue until $18,000 has been saved. At the age of 55 a minimum sum of $13,000 or the actual balance has to be retained in the Medisave account. Any surplus over the minimum amount may then be withdrawn and used for other purposes.

As its name suggests, Medisave is a savings scheme and not an insurance system. Money put into the scheme belongs to the individuals concerned and is not pooled. The aim is to create an incentive for citizens to build up sufficient reserves to meet treatment costs while avoiding the inappropriate use of services. Personal responsibility lies at the heart of this arrangement and is reinforced by the transfer of funds in savings accounts to relatives on death. Government subsidies fund part of the costs of health care but individuals must make some contribution to these costs, even for the most basic types of treatment.

Medisave is supplemented by two other schemes. Medishield offers protection against the costs of catastrophic illness while Medifund provides a safety net of last resort for people who are unable to meet medical expenses. These three schemes are intended to ensure that no citizen is deprived of basic medical care. Under this system, individuals who choose to pay extra are able to obtain a higher level of service and a private sector exists alongside the public sector to enable patients to exercise choice. The combination of individual responsibility and government subsidies helps to keep health care affordable while giving patients an incentive to use services appropriately. The principle of co-payment lies at the heart of the Singaporean system and is designed to limit demand by making patients cost-conscious. This is reinforced by knowledge that expenditure on health care is taken from individuals' own savings rather than from social insurance or tax funds.

The Medisave scheme is one element in the Central Provident Fund which in total takes 22 per cent of each employees' income with employers contributing 18 per cent. The major part of the Fund is used to provide individuals with access to resources for pensions, health care and education. Unlike the social security systems of most developed countries, this is a funded rather than a pay-as-you-go scheme. There are therefore fewer concerns about the long-run financial stability of the Central Provident Fund as contributions are designed to be sufficient to meet both medical care and retirement pension needs. It is recognised that the rate of contributions will have to increase as the population ages but the scheme has been established on the basis that the savings accumulated during working years will be sufficient to meet expenses in later life. Surpluses can be used for home buying and Singapore has one of the highest owner-occupancy rates in the world.

Government regulation extends to health service delivery as well as finance. Again this is motivated by recognition of market failure in health care and the need to avoid over-provision of services and cost escalation. Regulation covers the number of doctors, the degree of specialisation that is permitted (60 per cent of doctors work in primary care), the number of hospital beds, the provision of specialist facilities such as intensive care units, and the availability of tertiary services. Government also controls the prices that hospitals charge and the level of co-payments by patients.

One of the features of Singapore is the existence of different classes of hospital care. As an example, patients in public hospitals may choose one of four categories of care. Patients opting for the highest category of care receive no subsidy from the government and pay the full costs out of their own Medisave accounts. This gives them access to facilities such as air conditioning, privacy and choice of doctor and food. The government's aim is to move more of this care to the private sector, thereby enabling public hospitals to concentrate on offering a good basic level of service to middle- and low-income groups. It is anticipated that private hospitals will over time provide 30 per cent of acute hospital beds compared with 20 per cent at present and that these hospitals will cater increasingly for patients wishing to buy a higher level of service. The encouragement given to the private sector again illustrates the search for a middle way between state control and a free market in health care.

Singapore has been able to contain expenditure on health care by acknowledging the inevitability of rationing. As the recent white paper on health policy noted:

> We cannot avoid rationing medical care, implicitly or explicitly. Funding for health care will always be finite. There will always be competing demands for resources, whether the resources come from the State or from individual citizens. Using the latest in medical technology is expensive. Trade-offs among different areas of medical treatments, equipment, training and research are unavoidable. When public funds are involved, doctors have to decide which patients will benefit most from an expensive treatment. To get the most from a limited health budget, we need to exclude treatments which are not sufficiently cost effective to belong to the basic health package available to all. We must allocate resources according to rational priorities so that they can do the most good for the largest number of people.[1]

In practice this utilitarian principle means that the basic package of services is intended to offer treatment that is cost-effective and of proven value. It excludes services that are considered non-essential or cosmetic, experimental drugs and techniques whose effectiveness is not yet proven, and heroic efforts to keep people alive regardless of their quality of life and prospects of recovery. The basic package is defined in broad terms rather than fine detail and a great deal of discretion is left to doctors to decide when to carry out a procedure or to prescribe a drug. Services explicitly excluded from the package include *in vitro* fertilisation, gender reassignment operations, and heart, lung, liver and bone marrow transplants. Patients who can afford to may pay for these treatments in the private sector and in due course they may be added to the basic package. This will only occur, however, when there is sufficient evidence available of their cost-effectiveness.

Competition between hospitals is intended to stimulate efficiency and there is some evidence that this has worked in public hospitals.[2] However, private hospitals compete by offering the latest technology and equipment, leading to duplication of specialist facilities. Competition has also resulted in some doctors leaving public hospitals to work in the private sector. In response, public hospitals were forced to increase the renumeration of doctors, thereby adding to the cost of inflation. The white paper on health policy noted the need to strike a balance between competition and regulation, commenting: 'We must rely on competition and market forces to impel hospitals and clinics to run efficiently .... However, market forces alone will not suffice to hold down medical costs to the minimum'.

Outside hospital there is a choice between government polyclinics and primary care physicians who work privately. Patients usually pay the full cost of private treatment while the cost of treatment in polyclinics is subsidised by the government. Medisave funds cannot be used for this purpose. Primary care physicians do not have a list of patients and doctor-shopping is common. Competition between doctors helps to keep down charges which are typically around £9 per visit. This again illustrates the mixed approach to funding and delivery adopted in Singapore.

The health of the population reflects a strong commitment to public health and disease prevention. Expectation of life, infant mortality and other vital health statistics compare favourably with those of the United Kingdom, the United States and other developed countries.[3] Particular priority has been given to the reduction of cigarette smoking, the promotion of healthy lifestyles, health education and the school health service. Health improvements are also due in part to rising levels of per capita income resulting from rapid growth in the economy. Singapore has the sixth highest income per head of the population in the world, and the benefits are evident in the progressive gains in health that have been achieved.

The experience of Singapore has come under the microscope both in the United States, following the failure of the Clintons' health reforms, and in the United Kingdom as the Labour Party has started to explore options for the future of the welfare state. In the United States analysts trying to pick up the pieces from the demise of the Health Security Act have advocated the use of medical savings accounts as part of a new reform package. In the ensuing debate, the performance of the Singaporean health system has been the subject of lively discussion, with researchers offering different interpretations on whether the Singaporean model has succeeded or failed.[4]

In analysing the experience of Singapore, a number of cultural characteristics should be noted. These include the fact that Singapore is an immigrant country in which the population has not come to expect a state-funded welfare system to meet all its needs.

The population is also very young and the real test will come in the future as demographic trends match those found elsewhere. The government's plan is that when this happens the Medisave scheme will have matured to the point where reserves have built up to a level sufficient to meet the needs of an ageing population. A downturn in the economy or a changed attitude to work on the part of the next generation could turn these assumptions on their head.

The transferability of the Singaporean model is also affected by social values. The overriding importance of personal responsibility in Singapore stands in marked contrast to the traditional redistributive ethos of western European societies. Intragenerational accountability counts for more than inter-generational solidarity, suggesting distinct limits to the extent to which systems can cross national boundaries. Unless governments can alter attitudes towards welfare and the balance between personal and state action then there is little prospect of it finding favour in other countries.

In the United Kingdom, the Labour Party has drawn on the experience of Singapore to advocate the establishment of a stakeholder economy. In this respect, it should be noted that one of the benefits of the Central Provident Fund is the existence of cheap funds which have been used by the government to invest in industry and the economy. It is argued that this is one of the factors behind the high rates of growth seen in the Singaporean economy with welfare policy providing the basis for economic prosperity.

In fact, this is to reverse the logic of the Singaporean experience. It is because the economy has been so successful that the funding of welfare services has derived mainly from personal rather than government sources, thereby limiting the share of national income taken by public spending. The social authoritarianism of Lee Kuan Yew's government has transformed Singapore during the course of a generation through a combination of government regulation and individual effort. An economy which has grown by around 8.5 per cent a year since gaining independence and which provides full employment has enabled the government to require individuals to save to meet the costs of medical care, pensions and other needs. An economy with lower levels of employment would have had to rely much more on government funding, if only to provide a safety net for the poor.

The most important lesson therefore is that a stakeholder welfare system must grow out of a stakeholder economy rather than vice versa. If citizens feel valued through their employment and incomes then it may be possible to persuade or compel them to take greater responsibility for their welfare. If, on the other hand, they feel excluded from the economy and society, then there is no economic or moral basis for expecting them to take a stake in the system. Singapore has successfully appealed to its citizens' self interest by providing them with the means to participate fully in society. The means it has chosen may not meet with universal approval but it demonstrates clearly the basis on which a new social contract may be constructed. Put simply, the lesson for health policy makers from Singapore is sort out the economy first and the health care system will take care of itself.

From National Health Monopoly to National Health Guarantee

David G. Green

Summary

THE NHS is said to guarantee access to essential medical services for everyone and to create solidarity by 'integrating' the nation.

This essay argues that the government should continue to guarantee everyone access to medical care, but that it does not need to enforce a public-sector monopoly in order to do so. By requiring people to pay for health care, whether they are satisfied with the service they have received or not, the NHS takes away each consumer's bargaining power.

The task of government should be to empower consumers, not weaken them. Instead of assuming responsibility for both funding and provision, it should confine its role to tasks within its competence: above all regulation in the common good and ensuring that all, whether rich or poor, have access to the agreed standard of care.

The less-tangible argument—that the NHS integrates the nation—is often deployed as a smokescreen by the defenders of a centrally-directed social order, but the pursuit of solidarity should not be dismissed entirely. Social solidarity is desirable but can be achieved without creating a public-sector monopoly.

Two main policy recommendations are made. First, as part of a planned withdrawal from its monopoly role, the government should convert health authorities into independent mutual organisations whose task would be to act as champions of the consumer. They would provide information comparing the safety and efficacy of practitioners and hospitals and assist consumers in judging which insurers offer the best value for money. Second, hospitals should be restored to civil society as non-profit charitable trusts.

No less important, government should conceive the purpose of its withdrawal as, not so much the establishment of a market in the narrowest sense of creating room for commercial motivation in place of political motivation, but as creating the space for civil society to flourish. Use of the term 'civil society' rather than 'market' is intended to highlight the importance attached to non-commercial motivation in the supply of medical services. Of course, there will be competitive commercial activity, as there should be, but there is also a need to set free the other human motives that have in practice been predominant in medical care, not least mutual aid and benevolence.

INTRODUCTION

First, I will describe the current state of the debate; and second, I will outline an approach to the reform of medical services which tries to blend recognition of the special ethical priority of some medical treatment with respect for personal responsibility and choice.

The intention of the proposals is to transform the NHS from a national public-sector monopoly into a National Health Guarantee. The one redeeming feature of the NHS is that, formally, everyone, rich or poor, is protected. However, this desirable objective could be accomplished without state ownership of hospitals or the direct employment of medical staff. A better role for the government would be to provide universal access by means of a national guarantee, without attempting to provide health care through government agencies.

To that end, this essay argues that health care should be financed by insurance and suggests how a move to insurance might be brought about. In particular, the doctor-patient relationship would be improved if patients paid personally for health care (assisted by insurance) instead of having the cost forcibly taken from their pay packets in advance and paid to medical staff whether or not they have received reasonable care. A paying customer who has the freedom to go elsewhere can expect more attentive treatment, and that more care will be taken to explain treatment options. A patient whose money has been taken away at source has no such power. Today, patients are more aware than in the 1940s that there are personal choices to be made about the risks and benefits of medical treatment, and they wish to have the final say.

No less important, the essay argues that hospitals should be de-nationalised as non-profit community organisations similar to the voluntary hospitals before 1948.

THE CHANGING DEBATE

In the last few years there has been a dramatic change in the arguments deployed, not only by supporters of the NHS, but also by its critics.

Paul Starr, in his Pulitzer-Prize winning study, *The Social Transformation of American Medicine*,[1] identifies three radical changes that occurred during the 1970s: the crisis of affordability; the growing awareness that medical care was not always beneficial; and the recognition that competition and incentives had a part to play in overcoming some of the defects of the health care system. A fourth can be added: the rise of consumerism.

Affordability

In the 1940s there had been a feeling that there was a finite amount of ill-health to be cured so that the cost of the NHS would fall as people were restored to fitness. By the 1970s it was obvious that the cost of the NHS would be likely to rise for the foreseeable future. There were many conditions that showed no sign of final cure, including arthritis, diabetes, schizophrenia, Alzheimer's, coronary heart disease, cancers, and stroke. Improvements in technology made possible new treatments, previously unimagined, and as incomes rose, people tended to expect higher standards of care.

For many years the recognition that there were rising pressures on the NHS budget led to calls for more spending, but by the 1970s the underlying assumption that more medical care was inevitably a good thing was being challenged. Some demand was 'supplier-induced' and governments drew the conclusion that the more doctors and hospitals there were, the more medical interventions would be carried out. Consequently, they tried to control the number of medical personnel and to restrict the provision of hospitals and costly medical facilities.[2] Left-leaning academics like Professor Julian Le Grand of the London School of Economics argued that Britains's low expenditure as a proportion of GDP was a 'cause for celebration, not complaint'.[3]

Doubts About Medical Efficacy and the Medical Profession

There are two dimensions to growing doubts about medical efficacy. The first was inspired in Britain by Archibald Cochrane. In his 1971 book, *Effectiveness and Efficiency: Random Reflections on Health Services*,[4] he argued that doctors had a poor record of evaluating results, often relying on fashion, whim, or personal inclination. Many procedures did not work, or were unproven, or even caused iatrogenic disease. This line of criticism had many supporters within medicine, for it amounted to a re-assertion of the scientific method. It can be taken to extremes, for instance, by demanding a 'gold standard' of proof in the form of the randomised controlled trial, which usually takes the form of dividing a group of people suffering from a given condition into two groups, one of which will receive medication and the other an inert substance (or placebo). Neither the patient nor his own doctor knows who is receiving the placebo (hence the term 'double-blind' trial). This method, however, can not be deployed in all cases, not least because it is not ethically acceptable to withhold a treatment known to be effective from some patients (the control group receiving the placebo).

The line of criticism stimulated by Cochrane led to the modern movement for 'evidence-based' medicine and is reflected in the establishment of the Cochrane Collaboration, an international movement to gather and disseminate evidence about effective medical treatments.

The second critique was more radical. It was inspired in Britain by Thomas McKeown, whose *The Modern Rise of Population and the Role of Medicine* was published in 1976.[5] Medicine, he said, could take no credit for the decline in mortality since the mid-nineteenth century. The main factors were improved diet, as well as public health and hygiene measures. Today, critics in this tradition fight under the banner of 'health gain'. It is primarily a battle between doctors who deliver medical services and public-health specialists.

In addition to these critiques within medicine, doctors were also targeted by sociologists and political critics of the established (capitalist) order. Hostility towards the 'medical mafia' who ran the NHS was heightened by studies of inequality. The aim of the NHS had been equality, but inequalities had not been removed according to studies such as the Black Report of 1980. Some responded to the claim that the least well off were less healthy by blaming it on the concentration of medical facilities in wealthy London to the detriment of other areas. They advocated building new hospitals elsewhere. More radical critics saw this as 'moving deck chairs on the *Titanic*' and claimed that the health system could not hope to eradicate inequalities rooted in the very structure of capitalist society.

Sometimes the criticism of medicine took an extreme form that Starr calls 'therapeutic nihilism'.[6] Medicine, he said, had often been given unfair credit for health improvements, but now it was being 'disparaged without prudent regard for its benefits'.[7] Closely related was the argument of some socialists and 'lifestyle libertarians' that institutions such as schools, prisons and hospitals were methods of 'social control' imposed by bourgeois society.

Mental hospitals were their first serious target. Inmates were unfortunate people who had been labelled as deviant by a repressive society, when they were merely different. Thomas Szasz (*The Myth of Mental Illness*) and Erving Goffman[8] put the intellectual case, and popular films like *One Flew Over the Cuckoo's Nest* reinforced it. Society was sick; not the patient.

In his widely read book, *Medical Nemesis*, Ivan Illich argued that, not only did medicine often harm people, but the 'medicalisation' of life also destroyed the capacity of individuals for self-care and responsibility. Doctors had deliberately mystified medical knowledge, and 'colonised' natural events like childbirth and death, re-defining them as conditions requiring therapy and thereby destroying each individuals's ability to cope. Each advance of the medical empire required us to put our faith in professional therapists to the neglect of traditional institutions and rituals that have helped us to handle problems within families and neighbourhoods.

Ultimately, Illich favoured de-industrialisation, a remedy that has few adherents, but his critique of over-medicalisation has resonated with many reformers who were increasingly not willing to trust doctors. They sought to limit professional autonomy and demanded the de-institutionalisation and de-medicalisation of some conditions, especially childbirth and terminal illness. A demand for midwifery independent of the medical profession and the founding of the hospice movement were among the results.

Consumerism

The 1970s also saw the rise of consumerism. This development was a more radical departure in Britain than in America, where people had always been more inclined to think of themselves as consumers. From the 1960s and 1970s supporters of the NHS began to argue that health care was 'a right not a privilege' and to demand new rights, not so much of *access* to care but governing the *manner* in which health care was delivered. They wanted informed consent, the right to refuse treatment, to see their own medical records, and to participate in clinical decisions. Mental patients, in particular, demanded the right to a fair hearing before committal.

In the US the movement was intermingled with deep mistrust of a medical profession which was presented as wholly self-serving.[9] Consumers demanded that their interests were imposed by means of legal rights, and such rights were enforced by the US courts during the 1970s. The British courts were not so compliant but the same demands were voiced.

Competition and Incentives

The 1970s also saw the renewal of support for competition. Socialists typically saw the NHS as the pinnacle of their post-war achievement: it provided equal access for all to a necessity, 'integrated' the community, and allowed rational planning of health care facilities according to need rather than 'the market', which had been discredited as not only mistaken but wicked. Under the sway of the 'medical needs' paradigm, it was taken for granted that health care was an unequivocally good thing that should be equally available to rich and poor alike. This line of reasoning gave the NHS a distinct moral edge: everyone should have 'the best', with mere money no obstacle. In practice, this view was always a romantic exaggeration, for the NHS was inevitably a centralised system of rationed health care but, despite obvious failings, its founding objective of 'equal health care for all' enjoyed popular support and shielded it from the full blast of criticism.

Free-marketeers criticised the NHS as a public-sector monopoly which was inefficient in several senses: unit costs were high because there was no competition; investment in facilities was frequently misguided because of political interference, leading to the building of hospitals on the 'patch' of favoured politicians; and management of facilities was defective because old and unnecessary hospitals could not be closed. Demand had skyrocketed, leading to waiting lists and rationing of care, because there was no pricing: at zero price demand was said to be 'infinite'. Consumers were forced to pay for the NHS, but denied choice of service. It was pointed out that they could spend more on cars or holidays but were unable to increase the amount the NHS spent on their own health care. If they wanted to spend more they had to go private, which meant 'paying twice'. Organised medicine had been allowed to take advantage of public-sector monopoly to entrench its already formidable power. Consequently, consumers' interests were not given proper weight, reflected in long waiting times, waiting lists and crowded GPs' surgeries. Moreover, less-scrupulous consultants could manipulate waiting lists to increase their private practice. Inequality had not in fact been eliminated, because the articulate and well-spoken were able to obtain service at the expense of others: money no longer counted but 'knowing the ropes' did.

Free-market economists have typically advocated an insurance voucher scheme as an alternative to reliance on the allocation of a central budget from taxes. All would continue to pay taxes as usual, but each person would receive a health-insurance voucher sufficient to buy the basic package, and would be free to purchase additional services. In this way, the voucher would ensure access for all whilst also allowing consumers to signal their approval or disapproval of competing services through their spending decisions. Holders of vouchers would thus become paying customers rather than claimants. Providers would have to show more respect for customers, who would be able to go elsewhere if dissatisfied. Despite their considerable force, these arguments did not win the day in Britain.

However, in America, arguments for reform based on competition were taken seriously. Chief among those who restored the intellectual reputation of competition was Professor Alain Enthoven. He first proposed his Consumer Choice Health Plan in 1977 and during the ensuing years he has refined the argument substantially.[10] At the core of his approach is cost-conscious choice by consumers at the time they take out their insurance cover, not when they are being treated.

According to Enthoven, the medical care market as it operates in America suffers from market failures and for this reason an unfettered market is unsuitable and 'managed' competition necessary. But he does not go along with the anti-marketeers who offer up lists of market failures to support collectivist remedies. Lists of market failures, he says, describe 'problems to be overcome'. They are not necessarily reasons why a carefully designed system that uses market forces cannot work. And certainly they do not constitute a case for public-sector monopoly.

He takes particular exception to critics who contend that competition has been tried and failed in America and asserts explicitly that competition, as he understands the term, 'has not yet been tried in the US'. He argues cogently that American health care has not been competitive for many years because the American Medical Association (AMA) was able to impose its doctrine of 'guild free choice', an idea which appealed to American sentiment by purporting to offer choice whereas in reality it was a strategy for impeding competition by opposing the price competition encouraged by health maintenance organisations (HMOs) which enabled people to gain access to more cost-effective health care by opting to confine their choice to an approved panel of doctors.

Professor Enthoven's remedy for market failures is a system of 'managed competition', which has been amusingly characterised by his colleague, Richard Kronick, as 'giving the invisible hand a helping hand'.[11] The final section of this essay suggests how Enthoven's principles might be applied in Britain.

The New Rationale of NHS Supporters

From the 1940s until the 1980s, supporters of the NHS used to defend it as a means of guaranteeing equal access for all. Medical care was considered to be an unequivocally good thing that should never be denied. During the 1970s and 1980s, however, more and more intellectuals gradually began to support the NHS, not because they wanted more medical care for all, but because they mistrusted doctors and wanted to reduce the volume of medical treatment. The NHS was a 'sickness' service not a 'health' service, they argued, and resources should be diverted from medical interventions, which were often harmful or did no good, to public-health measures aimed at eliminating the root causes of ill health, such as air pollution, bad housing conditions, or poverty.

Having enjoyed the moral edge because its purpose was *more* health care for all, the NHS was now being justified as a method of empowering planners to provide *less* medical care. The starkness of the change of attitude was somewhat concealed behind demands for more 'health gain', but to the new generation of public-health enthusiasts, more 'health gain' did not mean more clinical care but higher public-health expenditure and fewer medical services. By the 1990s supporters of the NHS were drawing upon two distinct and contradictory paradigms: the old 'medical-needs' model, which retained considerable support, and the new 'public-health' approach.

By the 1990s, according to Wendy Ranade, a modern enthusiast for the public-health model, the 'heyday of the therapeutic era' had passed in favour of socio-ecological concepts of health.[12] The 1948 scheme gave priority to curative, hospital-based medicine at the expense of prevention, health promotion and community services; and treatment of short-term episodes of acute care were given priority over the rehabilitation of the chronically sick. Bevan had created a 'medical service not a health service', leaving medical privileges and the power of the teaching hospitals intact.[13]

The New Reasoning of NHS Critics

Critics of the NHS have also modified their views. During the 1960s and 1970s the lead was taken by economists who emphasised the incentive effects of competition, the signalling function of prices, and the attractions of consumer choice.

Subsequently, during the late 1980s and early 1990s, a new line of argument evolved, based largely on historical studies of what free-market health care had been like before the NHS. In Britain, hospitals were run either by local councils or by voluntary organisations, with acute care dominated by the voluntary hospitals. The strength of the voluntary tradition was, not its interest in maximising its return on capital, but its success in harnessing the best in people, whether in the form of professionals providing care, or individual members of the local community giving freely of their time and money to a good cause. To end public-sector monopoly by re-voluntarising hospitals would, therefore, be to terminate the running of hospitals by career politicians and public officials and to hand them over, not to profit-maximising corporations, but to non-government organisations like those that founded and ran the great voluntary hospitals until they were nationalised in 1948.

Similarly, primary care before the state took over was provided, not on narrowly commercial principles, but predominantly by consumer-led mutual aid organisations, namely the friendly societies covering about three-quarters of the population.[14]

Some economists have given the impression that the only approved motivation is commercial, a mistake criticised by Hayek, who drew attention to the importance of a third, independent, sector that was different from both government and commerce.[15] Moreover, the centrality of non-commercial motivation is possibly more relevant in health care than any other sphere. There have always been treatments that the poor could not afford, but which could not be withheld on moral grounds, and the issue in such cases has always been how others can best provide support. Before 1948, charitable and mutual principles were predominant and effective. Commercial activity played only a small part.

Nationalisation in 1948, in displacing 'the market', did not displace commercial activity but rather substituted political action for mutual and charitable activity. Thus, to defend competition instead of monopoly is not only to defend commercial motivation, but to advocate the full gamut of alternatives and especially the actual institutions preferred before political displacement: in particular, voluntary hospitals and consumer-led primary care.

MARKETS, CHOICE AND RESPONSIBILITY

The Internal Market

The Thatcher reforms announced in 1989 and introduced in 1990 used the 'market' language of incentives, prices and money following patients, but the main thrust was to increase the power of managers at the expense of doctors in order to improve cost-effectiveness. Market-like incentives, in other words, were being used as management tools in a centrally-directed service.

There is a division of opinion between free marketeers who see the internal market as a 'step in the right direction' and those who claim it has got the market 'a bad name without really trying it out'. In particular, some would say, the internal market reforms have reinforced the view of markets as concerned only with cost and commercial motives.

The 'internal market' has been called a 'defence industry procurement' model of competition, in which relatively few suppliers submit tenders or negotiate with a government agency. This produces results which are very different from a 'consumer sovereignty' model of competition in which the paying customer can choose from among a range of suppliers.

In a competitive market, prices serve two especially useful purposes. First, they create considered demand. Under a 'free' system, which in practice means one financed by compulsion, the consumer has no way of comparing the cost of health care with other desirable things, from consumer durables to the education of children. The compulsion removes responsibility for choice. Second, prices send signals to suppliers about the quantity and quality of care being demanded. This information enables them to judge how many facilities of various types to provide (on the experience of Britain, government planning of facilities has invariably led to rationing) and it tells producers whether or not people will pay more for higher standards. The 'prices' under the internal market serve far narrower purposes.

The case for the style of central direction on which the internal market is based has been defended by Professor A.J. Culyer. In a recent study, he begins by defining his objective in both technical and collectivist terms. The objective of a health system is to maximise 'health' and he takes it for granted that 'health' is to be maximised by politically-appointed authorities. Technically speaking, he says, the objective is 'efficiency' in the sense of choosing inputs that maximise intended outputs.[16] Economics, he says, has only 'one concept of efficiency' and 'central to this concept is the idea of maximising some value function, such as utility, welfare or health gain, subject to constraints'.[17]

In particular, he argues that if health maximisation is the objective, the system needs to be designed in order to 'maximise the appropriate use of cost-effective technologies'.[18] A fundamental question is: 'what is the optimum rate of diffusion of a new technology?' It is not adequate, he says, to reply, 'let the market decide', because 'the market is extremely imperfect'. He continues:

> In essence the problem involves a trade-off between two uncertain elements: the postponement of possible (but uncertain) benefits while effectiveness and cost-effectiveness trials and analyses are done, against the greater assurance that what is adopted will have real benefit and constitute value for money.

He says that he does not 'pretend to know' what the right general answer is, except that it is unlikely to be 'leave it to the market'.[19]

This argument suggests mistrust of personal preferences and a strong bent towards political control, presumably on the tacit assumption that a system of central direction is less prone to mistakes than a competitive market in which many people try out their ideas at once in the full glare of accountability.

Consider his remark that we cannot 'let the market decide'. He is speaking of 'the market' as if it were a person or an organisation (like the government) which reaches a decision after deliberation. But the statement 'let the market decide' is shorthand for a series of assumptions. No one knows for certain the optimal rate of diffusion of new technology; nor can anyone ever know for sure in advance what it might be or, indeed, whether it makes sense to assume that there is any such thing as an 'optimal' rate. Consequently, it is best to allow many people to try out alternatives in the hope of learning from their experience. It is precisely because of human imperfection that we 'let the market decide', that is we do not *decide* in the ordinary sense. We acknowledge our limited knowledge and rely on a social process combining trial-and-error and openness to contradiction to produce the best answers to date. As J.S. Mill remarked: 'The beliefs which we have most warrant for have no safeguard to rest on, but a standing invitation to the whole world to prove them unfounded.'[20]

Culyer says that he values market discipline on the supply side, but on closer examination he reveals a highly politicised view of 'the market' as an arrangement which can be designed in advance. The market is seen as a system of incentives and Culyer assumes that a market can be designed by technical experts who can create incentives to bring about desired behavioural end-results, defined as goals to be maximised. The relationship between inputs and these outputs is technical.

The danger in assuming that a system objective, such as 'maximising health', is a purely technical matter is that it can unduly alter the balance of power in favour of the medical authorities. NHS childbirth services provide an example. From the 1950s to the 1970s the declared objective of obstetricians was to save the lives of mothers and their babies. But under the guise of science in the service of saving life, medical power was used to induce births to fit the convenience of medical employees, with the result that there were more complications; and high-tech devices (such as foetal heart monitoring equipment) were deployed which, in some cases, caused clinical damage or increased complications. Many mothers have reported that, during those years, they were pressurised into accepting dubious medial advice. The professionals claimed that they were maximising health when they were not. Thus, on the experience of childbirth services, the acceptance of a prevailing orthodoxy imbued with the authority of science can enhance the capacity of decision makers to enforce their will against that of patients, and it can reduce the capacity of professionals to be self-critical or open to contradiction.

Health care plainly has much to do with skill, knowledge and science. But this scientific basis does not provide a rationale for the unchallenged authority of any given doctor. This is not only because medical knowledge and prevailing conceptions of 'best practice' are constantly changing, but also because much medical care has a non-scientific dimension—not least the importance of simple kindness, the alleviation of fear and the provision of comfort. The significance of the technical dimension can be, and has been, exaggerated.

To summarise: competition helps three kinds of discovery—the people in or out of a given market at any one time, the prices obtainable, and the products and services sought after. Prices tend to fall—not to marginal costs, but to the level that cannot at present be beaten by anyone else. Products or services tend to be those that purchasers want at present. The people producing in a given sector (rather than in another) are those who have provided what purchasers want (or who can afford to keep going in spite of not producing what consumers want at present). A competitive market is not a technical invention which allows pre-defined objectives to be met, but a system which allows scope for human ingenuity to design and re-design ways of improving our lives. It is based on the assumption that we are constantly learning. In particular, it rests on the belief that no authorities can set themselves up in advance on the basis of their training or expertise as the ones who should inevitably have the power of decision.

Can Consumers Choose?

Among the main reasons for hostility to consumer choice is paternalism, that is the view that consumers are not competent. Many economists analyse competition by employing the 'perfect competition' model. This model purports to describe the pre-conditions necessary for competition to work. In particular, it is said that there should be many suppliers (none of whom is big enough to determine the price) and consumers who are well informed about alternatives. If these conditions are not met, a market is not possible and a public-sector monopoly, or at least regulation, should be substituted.

As described earlier, the counter argument is that the competitive process is useful precisely because at any given moment we do not know who the best suppliers are, what prices will be charged, or what consumers know or want. All these 'facts' are in constant flux.

Consequently, well informed consumers are not a *pre*-condition for a market, without which a market cannot work. The vital function of competition is to *allow* consumers to become well informed by giving rise to the comparisons on which judgements can be based. To argue that a competitive market is not possible because consumers are not *already* well informed in practice leads to the continuance of monopoly, which puts them in an even weaker position.

The argument that consumers do not have the knowledge to choose is partly based on the failure to make a distinction between 'expertise in a given specialty' and 'expert knowledge as it relates to a particular case'. No potential patient has the time or inclination to learn all there is to know about the treatment of cancer. However, once he has contracted it, he does have an incentive to know as much as possible about his particular problem. Often it is possible for patients to acquire all the relevant knowledge about their condition. Indeed, it is frequently clinically advantageous that they should be well informed to ensure that they can give the doctor all the relevant information and protect themselves from misdiagnosis.

We do not all need to be experts in a given speciality; we only need to have mastered the essential facts, dilemmas and risks as they relate to our case. Health care systems should encourage, rather than discourage, education of that type.

Some medical decisions are complex, including risk/benefit trade-offs, but it is no answer to expect patients to 'leave it to the experts'. Rather, the majority of people should be encouraged to assume responsibility for these judgements. As Professor Culyer has argued, the weights given to the patient's and the doctor's opinions must vary according to circumstances.[21] There are some cases where the doctor's judgements are 'extremely marginal', for example, should the patient have a private room with bedside office facilities? In such cases, he says, assuming that having or not having these facilities is irrelevant to the medical outcome, there is every reason to permit free choice.

There are intermediate situations, for instance, 'should a woman have a Caesarean section?', and 'difficult decisions where there is a relatively low risk of a good outcome from a particular treatment and quite a high risk of a bad outcome'.[22] The doctor may be quite good at judging the *risk*, he says, but the patient is more expert at judging the *acceptability* of the risk.

Sometimes there are difficult trade-offs, for example, cancer of the larynx, where surgery may prolong life briefly but at the cost of the loss of voice, compared with non-surgical management which may involve a shorter life expectancy but use of the voice for longer.[23] At the other extreme are occasions when the patient is in no position to contribute to the decision, for instance, when he is unconscious and an immediate decision is required.

A common tactic of paternalists is to present themselves as defenders of the weak and frightened. What would happen, they say, to people too confused or frail to assume responsibility?

However, to put the vulnerable at the mercy of monopolists is no answer. To encourage them to believe that they should trust the doctor to whom they are assigned is the opposite of what is needed. Moreover, public sector monopoly makes escape from bad service more difficult. The weak and vulnerable are best protected by competition and by encouraging maturity and resourcefulness in other consumers. The more thoughtful consumers there are, the harder it will be for exploitative doctors to stay in the market at all. Competent consumers protect the interests of the frightened and frail as well.

Nevertheless, it is important not to leave matters to chance and, as an integral part of the reform of the NHS (to be described below), consumer organisations combining weak and strong consumers should be encouraged. The old friendly societies and some trade unions had committees that held doctors to account. In his autobiographical novel, *The Citadel*, A.J Cronin has described the doctor's fear of getting a visit from 'the committee' that ran the Tredegar Workmen's Medical Aid Society in South Wales. It was managed by thirty delegates, mostly miners. The presence of a committee meant that stronger characters were able to protect the weaker. There is no such system under the NHS, with the practical result that the strong can gain advantages for themselves at the expense of the weak.

For example, withholding or delaying treatment is one of the main problems of the NHS. An individual patient may make representations on his or her own behalf but, because the budget is limited, any gain will inevitably be at the expense of someone else. A complaint will only have wider value for the good of others if the protest leads to political demands. By contrast, individual demands for better or more care in a competitive environment are more likely to lead to feedback which will encourage providers to invest in new or improved facilities beneficial for all.

These are tendencies, not hard and fast rules, but it is likely that budget limits will create zero-sum situations. An American health maintenance organisation (HMO) in a competitive market may also under-serve patients, but if it receives complaints the HMO can raise prices or improve services. Diverse provision allows patients to compare what is available elsewhere for the same payment, so that there is an underlying dynamic encouraging responsiveness. In a famous analysis Hirschman deployed the alternatives of 'voice' and 'exit'.[24] He treated them as mutually exclusive alternatives when they are not. The key dynamic is 'voice' *backed* by 'exit'. Without exit, 'voice' is weaker and its effects are more likely to be confined to the few whose gain will be someone else's loss.

To sum up: NHS supporters have often argued that medical care is a need, not suitable for commercial provision, but it is increasingly being acknowledged that there is often an element of doubt about clinical decisions, not to mention some difficult trade-offs and that, consequently, the consumer has a part to play.

To what extent can consumers participate in medical decision-making? Some decisions—such as the non-medical comforts enjoyed in hospital—are for the consumer alone, but aspects of the clinical decision are also a consumer responsibility, not least whether a risk is worth taking. Moreover, since the cost is unavoidably a factor, leading inevitably to reduced standards in some cases, as even some NHS supporters acknowledge, then consumers should be as free as possible to influence decisions.

PROPOSALS FOR CHANGE

The alternative I will now defend is the renewal of 'civil society'. It could be called a 'market' view, but the term 'market' is often used in a narrow sense to mean 'commercial activity', and since this is not what I intend, I will prefer 'civil society', except where there is no ambiguity. The term 'civil society' includes a competitive market, but is wider.

The Argument So Far

When the NHS was founded its defenders argued that health care was an absolute need which should be met regardless of the cost. That is, they supported the NHS as champions of the poor, despite the fact that the poor were already covered by the voluntary and county hospitals.[25] During the 1980s they began to use a different argument, namely that medical treatment is often unnecessary or of unproven effectiveness. Therefore, they argued, doctors should be controlled by purchasing agencies appointed by the political authorities.

Alongside this rationale for controlling access, there is also the doctrine of 'health gain'. It defines the purpose of a health care system, not as caring for individuals who are ill, but as improving the health status of the nation or geographical area. The measure of success is not the number of individuals treated—cured, relieved of pain, assisted, supported—but the health status of the group, revealed by outcome measures such as mortality, behavioural indicators like smoking or alcohol consumption, and environmental measures such as air pollution. The NHS is dismissed as a sickness service not a fully-fledged health service. The Government has accepted some of this reasoning and set targets for the 'health of the nation'.[26]

Thus, in these two ways—gatekeeping, and redefining the aim of medical intervention in collectivist terms—supporters of public-sector monopoly pit themselves against the preferences of patients and the doctors who serve them.

Why Change is Necessary

Both the 1948 'needs' paradigm and the later 'health gain' tradition want state funding and public-sector monopoly (the 'needs' tradition in order to provide equal access; and the 'health gain' school because it wishes to control doctors' clinical habits and shift resources from medical services to public-health measures). But both neglect a fundamental characteristic of health care—the potential conflicts of interest between doctor and patient and doctor and purchaser.

Historically, the 'needs' school put people more at the mercy of doctors, as a result of the imposition of the panel system under the 1911 National Insurance Act and the nationalisation of the hospitals in 1948. Since the 1990 reforms, the 'health gain' enthusiasts have put both doctors and patients more under the control of purchasing agencies in the form of health authorities or commissions. Neither tradition has taken adequate precautions against doctors whose interests may clash with patients' or purchasers whose interests may clash with those of both doctors and patients. Because these conflicts are unavoidable, public-sector monopoly is the worst possible system for the provision of medical care.

Two particular defects in the NHS need to be overcome. First, the setting of an overall budget has harmful effects, especially the tendency for managers to stay within budget by lowering standards or withholding treatment, rather than by improving efficiency.[27] As Professor Enthoven has remarked, a global budget may seem desirable, but there is no certainty that the pressure will lead to improved efficiency:

> Competition is the way to achieve a system that is driven by the informed choices of consumers who are responsible for the cost consequences of their choices. A government controlled system is driven by political forces.[28]

Consequently, tight budgets do not necessarily bring about increased efficiency; they do a lot of collateral damage.

Second, because it is a public-sector monopoly—and thus by definition reduces competition—NHS doctors and managers have little incentive to serve consumers. The government has introduced the Patients' Charter to overcome this problem. But the minimum standards laid down by the Charter are a poor substitute for competition that allows patients real alternatives when dissatisfied.

Any reform of the NHS must involve insurance in some form, since some health care is expensive and unpredictable. There are two main possibilities: (a) a compulsory state system (national insurance); or (b) private insurance. On the Continent, national insurance allows a degree of consumer preference, but European governments tend to stipulate by statute the package of services that must be provided and impose global budgets on hospitals and doctors, so that the scope for cost-conscious consumer choice and responsibility is very limited. Compared with Britain, however, there is more diverse hospital ownership elsewhere in Europe, and it is widely accepted that competition has helped to raise standards of care.

A scheme based on private insurance would be feasible, and could be introduced by means of a voucher scheme or a tax credit to ensure universal access, but private insurers have come under heavy criticism and, in response, a new approach has been developed by Professor Alain Enthoven, usually called 'managed competition'. He intends that it will avoid, not only the worst effects of private insurance, but also of state-imposed global budgeting and public-sector monopoly.

Managed Competition

For Enthoven, the first aim of policy should be to encourage the empowered consumer, that is we should devise a system that encourages informed, cost-conscious consumer responsibility.

The government implicitly assumes that it can allocate a sum of money to the NHS sufficient to prevent the denial of needed care. But more or less every year since 1948 there have been funding crises leading to outright denial or delaying of needed treatments, some life-threatening. If individuals were allowed to decide how much of their own money to spend on health insurance, then the decision each year about how much to spend would be much better informed than a Treasury budget allocation, which has no relationship with needs or preferences. Insurance allows more subtle adjustments to be made from year to year in the light of experience because consumers can have a reasonable idea of what a change in premium will mean for the standard and range of care they will enjoy. The chief difficulty is that in all countries there is a poor minority who cannot afford medical care. However, this problem can easily be overcome.

Enthoven argues that a market made up on the one hand of suppliers, and on the other of individual purchasers acting alone, does not work well in health care. He gives four main reasons. First, insurers have a strong incentive to group customers according to their expected cost and to charge accordingly (experience rating or underwriting) with the result that costs are prohibitively high for some.

Second, healthy individuals have a strong reason not to insure—until they fall ill, when they hope to be treated free of charge because health care cannot ethically be withheld.

Third, the administration costs of insuring both individual policy holders and small groups can amount to 40 per cent of claims, making it prohibitively expensive.

Fourth, health insurance contracts, says Enthoven, are unnecessarily complex, thus making it difficult for consumers to make an informed judgement. Consequently, the insurance that works, he says, is group insurance with a 'sponsor'.

In the past I have defended opting out of the NHS to allow the gradual development of private alternatives.[29] Enthoven's proposal for sponsors as consumer champions involves a good deal of regulation, which may turn out to be excessive, but his scheme is a good compromise that meets the main objections put by critics of market competition whilst simultaneously allowing scope for the emergence of a competitive system. Moreover, the idea has already been tried elsewhere and found to work and, as Enthoven points out, it is compatible with 'limited government, voluntary action, decentralised decision making, individual choice, multiple competing approaches, pluralism, and personal and local responsibility'.[30] Despite the compromises involved, this is a long list of advantages.

In adapting Enthoven's scheme to Britain, I have had two particular objectives in mind. First, the new scheme should not put obstacles in the way of future improvement, but rather allow scope for human inventiveness and creativity. Over-regulation as much as monopoly can close off opportunities for the discovery of better ways of meeting human needs.

Second, the initial system should be based on experience of what has happened in the past when competition has been permitted. As Enthoven has shown, his model has been tried and tested in parts of America. There are examples of such systems in operation in California, including the California Public Employees Retirement System (CalPERS) covering 870,000 people[31] and the Stanford University employee scheme.[32] The State of Minnesota Group Insurance Program[33] is similar, and so too is the Federal Employees Health Benefits Plan in Washington, DC.

No less important, in Britain before the NHS consumers organised themselves in mutual organisations or friendly societies to provide medical care. Enthoven's model, therefore, draws on both modern US experience, and historical evidence of what medical care in 'civil society' actually looked like. Enthoven says that his proposals are not a free market.[34] However, if a free market were allowed to function for long enough, past experience suggests that it could well end up looking something like Enthoven's scheme. When not prevented from doing so by professional monopoly or unwise political intervention, earlier generations of consumers did obtain their care as members of organised groups precisely to even up the balance of power between the isolated individual and organised medicine. Moreover, from time to time they experimented with fee-for-service and invariably abandoned it.[35] Thus, creating a voluntaristic system does not entail blind faith in economic theory, but is based on what has worked in the past and what works today.

Outline of Enthoven's Scheme

Enthoven's scheme comprises four main elements.

1 Each year consumers choose a comprehensive care package for one year.

2 This consumer choice should be cost conscious, that is, part or all of the cost of the premium should be met by all individuals except the absolutely poor.

3 Providers should compete in economic units which integrate provision and insurance, either by establishing a single system, such as a health maintenance organisation (HMO) or by creating structures based on contracts between insurers and independent providers, such as preferred provider organisations (PPOs).

4 Agencies, which could be private organisations, or statutory bodies insulated from the political process, should facilitate consumer choice by offering comparative information about quality and price and by filtering out unsatisfactory insurers who try to compete by selecting good risks rather than encouraging cost-effective care.[36] Enthoven has given these intermediaries various names over the years, the latest of which is 'health insurance purchasing co-operative' (HIPC).

The relevant 'price', insists Enthoven, is not the cost of any given medical procedure, but the annual insurance premium, because it gives the consumer a reason to think about the total cost and to try to minimise it. Consumers must be price conscious at the time of taking out the insurance package, and in a position to compare packages. To facilitate comparisons providers should be required to price equal packages, so that during the open-enrolment season of about four weeks every year systematic comparisons can be made, comparing like with like. Enthoven is anxious that consumers should not have to choose between lists of covered and non-covered items, because it is an almost impossible choice for individuals to make with any confidence.

Implementation in Britain

How could a scheme like this be implemented in Britain?

The major difference between Britain and America is that British employers are not so heavily involved in health care. In America Enthoven expects employers to assume the 'sponsor' role in addition to area-based HIPCs. Other American enthusiasts for Enthoven's scheme, such as Paul Starr, prefer a more predominant role for area-based purchasing co-operatives. In Britain, the area-based model would probably be the best first step. We could build, for instance, on the existing health authorities by transforming them into purchasing co-operatives. The following measures would be necessary:

1   Health authorities should become purchasing co-operatives independent of government. They should be mutual organisations run by boards representing members.

2   Each year, purchasing co-operatives should invite private insurers to submit tenders for a comprehensive package of cover for anyone within their area. All insurers should be required to price a standard contract to facilitate value-for-money comparisons; to reduce market segmentation based on the range of services covered rather than on price or quality; to guarantee no hidden gaps in coverage; and to prevent risk selection reducing incentives to produce value for money. This standard package should be defined by each co-op to reflect members' preferences and to facilitate comparisons between co-ops.

3   Every person should have subsidised access to the lowest-priced plan that meets designated standards of quality and coverage. Subsidies should be paid by central government from taxes, but people choosing higher-priced plans should pay in full any excess over the price of the cheapest plan.

4   Consumers could make their choice once a year, based on the quoted prices and any comparative information supplied by the co-ops. They could have, say, four weeks to consider the options and notify their decision to the co-op. Individuals should notify their choice to the co-op and not direct to the insurer to avoid covert selection of low-risk subscribers.

5   In the first year, the Treasury should apportion an amount per person based on the previous year's NHS expenditure. After the first year, the Treasury allocation should be based on the market price for the standard package, although the exact method will need to be the subject of consultation. One approach would be to define a national standard package and to base the Exchequer subsidy on its market price. However, if co-ops are to offer different standard packages, as they should, it will be more difficult to calculate the subsidy. One method of overcoming this difficulty might be to base the subsidy on the average price of a

selection of ten or so different packages, chosen to reflect regional variations.

6   There should be continuous coverage, to prevent insurers from dumping costly subscribers.

7   There should be community rating, that is the premium ought to be the same regardless of the health status of the individual, though age rating would be acceptable.

8   No one should face exclusions or limitations of coverage because of pre-existing conditions.

9   Co-ops should be allowed to exclude some insurance companies or plans if they do not comply with the standard package. Co-ops would also mediate in disputes between consumers and insurers, and publish information about complaints against hospitals, providers or insurers.[37]

10   To assist consumers to make well-informed decisions, the purchaser co-operatives should provide information comparing prices, standards and hospital and provider performance. They should also have a duty to disseminate the results of clinical and epidemiological studies of efficacy and cost-effectiveness.

11   To encourage competition, existing NHS hospitals should be removed from political control by privatising them as non-profit, voluntary hospitals.

12   GP fundholders could continue in being, but they would be among the choices available to individuals. They would have to price the standard package like other insurers and bear the full risk involved.

Enthoven strongly argues that co-ops should adjust risks between plans because, either by accident or design, risks will tend to fall unequally on insurers. He proposes estimating the total risk for the sponsored population (based on age, sex, disability status and diagnosis). Each plan would then be assigned a weight. For example, a plan with costs expected to be one per cent above the whole-group average, would be assigned a weight of 1.01. A price would be attached to each percentage point of expected cost—perhaps one per cent of the premium of the lowest-priced plan—and surcharges applied to plans with low expected costs and subsidies to those with high. These adjustments would be made after individuals had made their choice of insurer, so that the 'risk pool' of each insurer was known. The adjustment should be set so that it does not pay insurers to use 'plan design' or other methods to avoid high-risk consumers. Thus, a company with expected costs of two per cent below the whole-group average might receive 98 per cent of the lowest premium, and one with expected costs five per cent above the average, would receive 105 per cent.

This last recommendation is one of the most controversial parts of Enthoven's proposal because it is very difficult to estimate from the known characteristics of subscribers what their costs will be over the ensuing 12 months. As Enthoven concedes, this is true even of subscribers who have a condition such as AIDS or HIV. Moreover, demographic variables identify only a small amount of the variation in costs between individuals.[38] The RAND Health Insurance experiment, for instance, found that one per cent of patients in a given year accounted on average for 28 per cent of the total cost. Most of these patients could not be identified in advance.

Because of these difficulties it would be desirable to establish a trial scheme for 2-3 years, in the hope of placing risk adjustment on a more sound technical footing.

There are some dangers to be avoided. For the purchasing co-operative to be an honest broker, it must not have its own insurance plan.[39] Moreover, it is very important that health authorities should not also be planning agencies, controlling investment in medical facilities. Such planning is best accomplished by competing providers. Enthoven's proposal enjoys bipartisan support in America and Paul Starr, who is among the left-leaning supporters, is emphatic that purchasing agencies should not be planning agencies. Their task is to be the champion of patients' interests and to foster and facilitate informed and responsible consumer choice. To give them a planning role, he says, would be to create a potential conflict of interest between their advocacy and planning duties.[40]

Thus, the resulting system would work something like this. Each existing health authority would become a purchasing co-operative. It would not provide medical services and would have no role in planning medical facilities. Its task would be to ask private insurers to price the same comprehensive package of care, initially equivalent to the care provided by the NHS. After the first year, the payment by the Treasury to each co-op would be based on the cheapest standard package in each locality (or the average for a selected sample). Anyone choosing to pay more would do so with their own money. There is no way of deciding in advance what this basic package should be, it can only be discovered from experience. Thus, we would continue to pay taxes as now, but a sum of money equivalent to the lowest-priced plan would be paid by the government to co-ops on behalf of all members. Everyone, rich or poor, would be included.

Hospitals would charge insurers for their services, just as they charge health authorities now. Private hospitals, whether for-profit or not, would compete on equal terms. All hospitals would be free to enter into contracts or arrangements with insurers as they believe best. Similarly, GPs would charge insurers or offer pre-paid services.

Initially the scheme would be based on existing health authorities, but as under Enthoven's scheme, it should be possible to establish mutual purchasing agencies other than area-based co-operatives. According to Enthoven, the RAND Health Insurance Experiment found that groups of 10,000 or more have administrative costs of 5.5 per cent, whereas for smaller groups it can be 40 per cent.[41] Thus, a group of 10,000 is large enough to secure the relevant economies of scale. Consequently, it should be possible to establish alternative mutual or stakeholder purchasers so long as no fewer than 10,000 individuals subscribe. This would create competition between co-ops and permit consumers to escape from their local co-op if it proved to be a bad performer. Such competition would, in a sense, create a series of competing regimes regulating health insurers.

It can be expected that insurers/providers will take a variety of forms. Some will offer restricted lists of hospitals and special-ists, and others a wide variety. One of the dangers in any system is local monopoly. Under this scheme local monopoly power would be diminished, whereas under the NHS internal market some health authorities restrict choice of specialist to the hospitals with which they have contracts. It can be to the advantage of consumers to restrict their choice in order to increase their control over the providers they have selected. HMOs and PPOs, for instance, are based on freely-chosen limitation of choice, but to choose restriction is quite different from having it imposed by a health authority. The outcome of the proposed system would be a widening of choice and a reduction of local monopoly power.

An Example

How might such a scheme affect a family of say, a man, wife and two children? If we assume that the cost of the cheapest standard package for a family of four is £2,600 per year, then this amount would be paid by the government to the co-op. The family would choose its insurer and, if it chose a company charging £3,000, it would pay the difference of £400 to the co-op. However, the insurer would not necessarily receive £3,000.

The insurer may a have a low risk profile estimated at 95 per cent of the average for all co-op members. If its risk profile was equivalent to the average it would receive £3,000 from the co-op (made up of £2,600 subsidy and £400 from the consumer). In this example, however, it receives 95 per cent of £2,600 (£2,470) plus £400 from the consumer.

Another approach would be for the government to assign a tax credit of £2,600 to the family and for them to pay the whole £3,000 to the co-op. For families with a tax liability above £2,600, this measure would have the merit of allowing the family to keep their own earnings, thus diminishing the involvement of the government. For those with a tax liability below £2,600 a tax credit would be paid, reducing with earnings. People with no earnings would receive the full £2,600 in the form of a voucher.

Under such an arrangement universality of access would be preserved but a higher degree of price consciousness and a bigger sense of ownership of the co-op would be encouraged.

Conclusion

A system of purchaser co-operatives would guarantee access for all without public sector monopoly, create mutual organisations that could become the focus for social solidarity, and allow private organisations the freedom to discover better ways of meeting our needs and to harness the best in human nature.

Notes

Editor's Introduction

1 Klein, R., *The Politics of the NHS*, London: Longman, 1983, p. 1.
2 Williams, P.M., *Hugh Gaitskell*, Oxford: Oxford University Press, 1982, p. 183.
3 Cmnd. 663, *Report of the Committee of Enquiry into the Cost of the National Health Service*, London: HMSO, 1956.
4 OECD, *The Reform of Health Care: A Comparative Analysis of Seven OECD Countries*, Paris: OECD, 1992.
5 Griffiths, R., *The NHS Management Inquiry Report*, London: DHSS, 1983.
6 Cmnd. 555, *Working for Patients*, London: HMSO, 1989.

Why Health Care Should Be Provided Free at the Point of Service

1 Robinson, R. and Le Grand, J. (eds.), *Evaluating the NHS Reforms*, London: King's Fund Institute, 1994.
2 Blaxter, M., *Health and Lifestyles*, London: Tavistock, 1990.
3 Davey, B., Gray, A. and Seale, C., *Health and Disease: A Reader*, Buckingham: Open University Press, 1995.
4 Marmot, M., Shipley, M. and Rose, G., 'Inequalities in death —specific explanations of a general pattern', *The Lancet*, Vol. 1, 1986, pp. 1003-06.
5 Marmot, M. and Davey Smith, G. 'Why are the Japanese living longer?', *British Medical Journal*, Vol. 299, 1989, pp 1547-51.
6 Wilkinson, R., 'Income distribution and life expectancy', *British Medical Journal*, Vol. 304, 1992, pp. 165-68.
7 Titmuss, R., *Commitment to Welfare*, London: Allen and Unwin, 1968.
8 Gough, I., *The Political Economy of the Welfare State*, Basingstoke: Macmillan, 1979.
9 Beattie, A., Gott, M., Jones, L. and Sidell, M., *Health and Wellbeing: A Reader*, Basingstoke: Macmillan Press Ltd.,1993.
10 World Bank, *Investing in Health*, World Development Report, New York: Oxford University Press, 1993.

Co-payment—A Vehicle for NHS Funding Enhancement?

1 Laidlaw, D. *et al.*, 'The Sight Test Fee: effect on ophthalmology referral and rate of glaucoma detection', *British Medical Journal*, Vol. 309, 1994, pp. 634-36.

Learning from the Tigers

1 Republic of Singapore Ministerial Committee on Health Policies, 'Affordable health care: a white paper', Singapore: Ministry of Health, 1993.

2 Hsiao, W.C., 'Medical Savings Accounts: lessons from Singapore', *Health Affairs*, 1995, pp. 261-66.

3 Ministry of Health Singapore, *Annual Report*, Singapore: Ministry of Health, 1994.

4 Hsiao, W.C., *op. cit.*; Massaro, T.A. and Wong, Y., 'Positive experience with medical savings accounts in Singapore', *Health Affairs*, 1995, pp. 267-72.

From Monopoly to Guarantee

1 Paul Starr, *The Social Transformation of American Medicine*, New York: Basic Books, 1982.

2 See for example Abel-Smith, B., *et al.*, *Choice in Health Policy: An Agenda for the European* Union, Aldershot: Dartmouth, 1995, p. 44.

3 *New Statesman*, 29 January 1988, p. 12.

4 London: Nuffield Provincial Hospitals Trust, 1971.

5 McKeown, T., *The Modern Rise of Population and the Role of Medicine: Dream, Mirage or Nemesis?*, Rock Carling Monograph, London: Nuffield Provincial Hospitals Trust, 1976.

6 Starr, *op. cit.*, p. 408.

7 *Ibid.*, p. 410.

8 *Asylums*, Harmondsworth: Penguin, 1968.

9 Starr, *op. cit.*, p. 392.

10 Enthoven, A., 'The history and principles of managed competition', *Health Affairs*, Supplement 1993, pp. 24-48.

11 R. Kronick, 'A helping hand for the invisible hand', *Health Affairs*, Spring 1994, pp. 98-101.

12 Ranade, W., *A Future for the NHS?: Health Care in the 1990s*, London: Longman, 1994, p. 152.

13 Ranade, *op. cit.*, pp.9-10.

14 Green, D., *Working-Class Patients and the Medical Establishment*, London: Gower, 1985.

15 See Hayek, F.A., *Law, Legislation and Liberty*, London: Routledge, 1979, vol. 3, p. 50.

16 Culyer, A.J., 'Chisels or Screwdrivers? A critique of the NERA proposals for the reform of the NHS', in Towse, A. (ed.), *Financing Health Care in the UK: A Discussion of NERA's Prototype Model to Replace the NHS*, London: OHE, 1995, p. 24.

17 *Ibid.*, p. 27.

18 *Ibid.*, p. 29.

19 *Ibid.*, p. 26.

20 Mill, *On Liberty*, London: Dent, 1972, p. 83.

21 Culyer, *op. cit.*, p. 34.

22 *Ibid.*, p. 34.

23 *Ibid.*, p. 34.

24 Hirschman, A.O., *Exit, Voice and Loyalty*, Harvard: Harvard University Press, 1970.

25 Prochaska, F., *Philanthropy and the Hospitals of London: The Kings Fund, 1897-1990*, Oxford: Clarendon Press, 1992.

26 *The Health of the Nation*, Cm 1523, London: HMSO, 1991.

27 The Treasury assigns a budget for the NHS, but non-fundholding GPs are not subject to cash limits, though they are under financial constraints and spending on pharmaceuticals is not cash limited, but there are 'target budgets'.

28 Enthoven, A.C., 'The history and principles of managed competition', *Health Affairs*, Supplement 1993, p. 41.

29 *Everyone a Private Patient*, London: IEA, 1988.

30 Enthoven, *Health Affairs*, Supplement 1993, p. 46.

31 *Ibid.*, p. 37.

32 Enthoven, A., 'The effects of managed competition' in Helms, R.B., *Health Policy Reform: Competition and Controls*, Washington: AEI, 1993, pp. 218-27.

33 Feldman, R. and Dowd, B., 'The effectiveness of managed competition in reducing the costs of health insurance', in Helms, R.B., *Health Policy Reform: Competition and Controls*, Washington: AEI, 1993, pp. 176-217.

34 Enthoven, *Health Affairs*, Supplement 1993, p. 44.

35 Green, D.G. *Working-Class Patients and the Medical Establishment*, Aldershot: Gower, 1985, p. 130.

36 A.C. Enthoven, *Theory and Practice of Managed Competition in Health Care Finance*, Amsterdam: North Holland, 1988; A.C. Enthoven and S.J. Singer, 'A single-payer system in Jackson Hole clothing', *Health Affairs*, Spring 1994, pp. 81-95.

37 Enthoven, *Health Affairs*, Supplement 1993, p. p. 36.

38 *Ibid.*, p. 34.

39 *Ibid.*, p. 35.
40 Starr, P., 'Design of health insurance purchasing co-operative', *Health Affairs*, Supplement 1993, p. 60.
41 Enthoven, *Health Affairs*, Supplement 1993, p. 35.